Phosphorescence

Phosphorescence

POEMS BY MARY CARLTON SWOPE

Word Poetry CINCINNATI

Published by Word Poetry
P.O. Box 541106
Cincinnati, OH 45254-1106

ISBN: 9781625493651

Poetry Editor: Kevin Walzer
Business Editor: Lori Jareo

Visit us on the web at
wordpoetrybooks.com

ACKNOWLEDGMENTS

The author is grateful to the editors of the following publications in which some of these poems appeared, often in earlier versions.

13th Moon, Winter 1975. "Leaving"; Volume II No. 2.: "Soap Opera," "Loaded."

Anthology of *Magazine Verse & Yearbook of American Poetry:* 1981 Edition, edited by Alan F. Pater. Copyright © 1981 by Monitor Book Company, Inc."Couple."

The Book of Falmouth: A Tricentennial Celebration: 1686–1986, Mary Lou Smith, editor. Copyright © 1986, Falmouth Historical Commission, Publisher. "Phosphorescence."

Center Pieces: Selections from Workshops at the Writer's Center, 1977-1980. Copyright ©1981 The Writer's Center. "The Search."

Dark Horse: Boston's first poetry and fiction newspaper. Winter Issue: No. 20, 1979. Copyright © 1979 Dark Horse Poets Cooperative: "Couple," "A Woman's Place."

The Ear's Chamber: 50 Metro Poets. SCOP Publications, Inc. College Park, MD. Copyright © 1981: "Texas Falls."

The House, That Octopus: Poems by Mary Swope, Copyright © September, 1981 by PeKaBoo Press, Falmouth, MA. Eric Edwards, editor. "After," "Before," "The House That Octopus," "Mending," "Weekend Homecoming."

Montpelier Plus 4: 1980-1984 edited by Karen L. Arnold, Copyright © Montpelier Cultural Arts Center, 1984: "Secrecy."

National Poetry Competition Winners 1984: Chester H. Jones Foundation: "Open."

New England Poetry Calendar and Engagement Book, 1983. Copyright © 1982 by Yellow Umbrella Press (Chatham, MA). "The Foggy Bottom Morris Men Dance for the Economy," "Putting Away the Boat."

Poetry, July 1961, Vol 98 Number 4: "Of Tutankhamen's Tomb." (Mary Carlton)

The Poet Upstairs: A Washington Anthology Edited by Octave Stevenson. Copyright © 1979 Washington Writers' Publishing House. "Gesture," "Loaded."

Radcliffe Quarterly: Copyright ©Radcliffe College, 1979, 1984, 1986. "My Mother Said," "Ironing," "Organ Recital" ("Bacchanal for the New Organ.")

The Runner magazine, Copyright © 1979. "Waking Woods Hole,"

Stone Country Vol. 7 No 2: Copyright © 1980 by Judith Neeld. "Putting Away the Boat."

Summer Poems, 1960 No. 2 & 10. "After" ("Reply to an Unasked Question"), "The Wall."

Woods Hole Reflections, Mary Lou Smith, editor Copyright © 1983, Woods Hole Historical Collection, Publisher.: "Waking, Woods Hole;" "North Wind Sonnet."

DEDICATION: IN MEMORIAM

WINSLOW CARLTON, my father,
who sang and swam with us
MARGARET GILLIES CARLTON, my mother,
who read poems aloud and created bedtime stories
and her brother, DONALD GILLIES,
who died too young
but left me a legacy of poetry, theater
and a love of the Scottish Highlands and its people

APPRECIATION:

To ALICE KOCIEMBA, without whom this collection would have
never been completed and RICH YOUMANS, who introduced me
to the *haibun* form and created the haiku for *"Tracks."* I shall be
eternally grateful to my cousin-in-law, JULIA SWOPE CHILD, for
the beautiful drawings that enhance this volume. Thanks also
to my niece MARGARET CARLTON-FOSS, a patient guide through
the thorny forests of ever-changing computer software on
the path to formatting this collection, and her diplomatic
suggestions as a fellow poet and writer.

To CAROLINE KNOX for a longstanding friendship, begun at
Harvard, renewed of late by our common fascination with
language and her cool humor. I am especially grateful for her
encouraging comments and suggestions on an early draft of
this book. To VIEVEE FRANCIS for offering the manuscript a final
review and for suggesting that the title poem act as the fulcrum
of the book, not its ending, and to our mutual friend, SALLY
BRADY, fine writer, teacher and lifelong friend, who introduced
us and has rescued me more than once. It was she who
introduced us to Michael Russem, who designed this collection.

To ERIC EDWARDS, who in 1981 published a charming eight-page
chapbook of my poems.* To my sister SAMM CARLTON, who
encouraged me to return with her to the joy of writing poetry,
and to join STEEPLE STREET POETS, who welcomed me warmly
to their workshop in Mashpee and continue to inspire me.
To our younger sister, RHONA CARLTON-FOSS, a gifted teacher
and writer, who has always had the happy illusion that I can
do anything. To CAROL BURNES, sister in art and soul, poet,
storyteller, intuitive teacher, who helps me dig deeper.

The House, That Octopus, PeKaBoo Press © 1981, Eric Edwards, publisher

To poet and teacher RUTH WHITMAN, and the fine Cambridge poets who brought their amazing work and insights to her Harvard Extension Course in the 1960s, a place of joy and discovery because of her warmth and wisdom. My thanks to KATHLEEN SPIVACK, friend and colleague, whose workshops helped to free me from my comfort zone.

I am fortunate to have had many friends among Washington, DC's thriving poetry community, remembering especially the late KATHERINE ZADRAVEC, whose poems and friendship I will always cherish, and whose idea it was that SCOP Publications should create an anthology of "car poems."* I am grateful to STACY TUTHILL for inviting me to join SCOP's editorial board and spend happy times working with dedicated colleagues on a few of the handsome books produced under her leadership. Warm thanks also to JEAN NORDHAUS and LINDA PASTAN for their friendship and support, and to the POETRY COMMITTEE at the Folger Shakespeare Library. Many thanks to AL LEFKOWITZ and others for creating a welcoming community at the WRITERS CENTER in Glen Echo Park.

To my many friends at Harvard, including those I joined on the Editorial Board of the ADVOCATE; especially my beloved tutor, BILL ALFRED. To my teachers at THE BREARLEY SCHOOL, where I was fortunate to receive my first twelve years of education, who occasionally let me hand in poems instead of essays but also taught me the value of discipline and rigor. ANNE LLOYD BASINGER was an early influence there in creative writing, encouraging us to write original plays and original stories based on Ancient History. Special gratitude is due to JEAN NEVIUS, a fierce Viking presence, adored by many, who took poetry seriously and expected her students to do the same. When I was twelve, she found books of poems in the school library

*American Classic: Car Poems for Collectors, Mary Swope and Walter L. Kerr, Editors.©1985 SCOP Publications, College Park, MD

she thought I would enjoy, and later encouraged a group of her students to subscribe to concerts and readings at The Poetry Center of New York's 92nd Street YMHA then joined us to hear the major poets of the age read from their works, from which I gained an appreciation of the voices and forms of mid-century 20th Century poetry. I will never forget hearing Dylan Thomas and his small band of American actors perform his 'play for voices,' *Under Milkwood*, as part of that extraordinary series.

Finally, I want to express love and gratitude to my family for putting up with what my sweet husband, Gerry, called my "busy life:" a life that in early May he left me to continue on my own, but with the caring support of our two sons, Tim and Ian, their spouses Patti and Jennifer, and our grandchildren Fiona and Malcolm.

MARY SWOPE *July, 2020*

CONTENTS

mirror

appetite

wall

carapace

deep waters

wings

waking

mirror

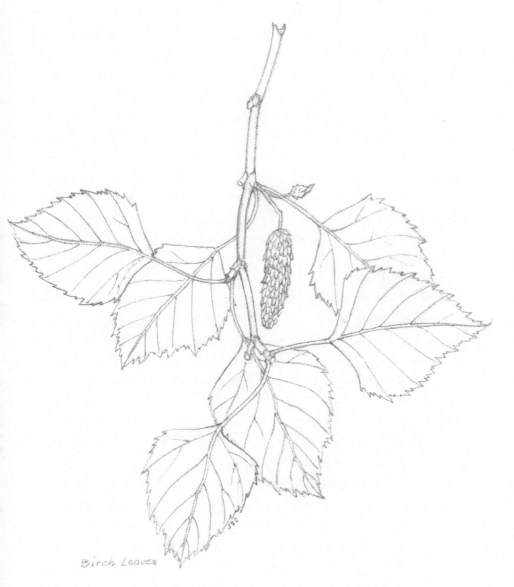

Birch Leaves

Before

Before she can begin she must sharpen her pencil
but before that she must find the pencil and
empty the drawer where pencils are kept
find the name of the store that sells brass
key rings a name she looked up the last time
she emptied the drawer of keys which she
placed in the green ashtray (still waiting)
phone the storekeeper to find if he still stocks
brass key rings so she can buy one put her
keys on it clear the desktop dig out the pencil
sharpener from under the rubber bands
sharpen the pencil when she finds it and begin

Gesture

A young girl kneels
by the roadside—books
under the crook of one arm
she strokes a small shining dog

I see her caught
in the copper & blue afternoon
a girl in marble
tying her sandal

long brown hair
across one cheek falls
down her white blouse—brilliant
in the perfect air

I see her through my car window
through the rushing
hour—dark sand streaming
down the glass

Above her a birch
unwraps itself
peels off layers like
bells, like a gift

Mirror

I once knew how to make a shoe-box world
so real it seemed that everything I knew
(or cared for) followed pebbled paths that curled
across a tiny landscape starred with dew.
A pocket mirror could become a sea
or just a winter pond to skate across
by piling edge and corner with debris
or cotton-wool, glued loosely to the glass.

Then two things happened: cotton became snow
—or sand that formed low dunes along a shore—
and the strict surface stirred, as far below
dark under ice, I heard the swell and roar.
Now, making worlds of words and images,
I know too well how flat a mirror is.

My Mother Said

Darling, but you're not wearing that, she said.
is that where you do your homework
—lying on the floor? Why don't you
brush your hair! Look at this room!

She said, *That's very nice, dear,*
for an eight-year old,
Yes, I'm listening. Yes, yes
I hear you. I'm sure they
like you. Well, girls like girls
who look neat, who are well-
organized. You're not very
well-organized, are you, dear?

Years later, when I asked, woman to
woman, if she'd had a lover
before she married Dad, she said,
What a personal question! Hard for a mother
to answer:If I didn't, I'm old-fashioned,
If I did, what kind of example do I set my daughter?

And all the while
she was reading Ouspensky,
studying the mystics, practicing
meditation, and all the while
she was on the telephone
running things she didn't want to run.

Don't waste yourself.
You only have one life,
my mother said.

The Secret

The dentist looked to me, at ten,
like pictures of Governor Dewey:
dark wavy hair, a moustache. The minty smell
from the sugarless gum he always chewed
made me shrink in the chair. He wore
a starched, white coat that pressed
against me as he worked on my mouth.
It won't hurt, he promised, but it
always hurt. One day he needed
to take an X-ray of my teeth. Now, that
was interesting! He asked if I could keep
a secret. Of course I could! He let me
join him in the tiny darkroom where he
developed the X-rays. I must have looked
at the x-rays, hanging in the red light. He put my hand
on the bulge at the front of his trousers, a funny thing
to do, a funny secret to keep. I had
lots of cavities. He'd wink at me as I lagged
into his office. *Remember our secret*, he 'd breathe,
wetly. I finally told my sister. She never could
keep secrets.

Fat Daughter

My mother was bigger
when I was younger
now I am bigger but she
is stronger
Soft she held me
I stormed I thundered
She tightened hardened
I grew like a blunder
Swelling ballooning
I filled the sky

Follow your nature
carolled my mother
Bobbing tugging
I sailed the wind
Listen! I shouted
That's the wind talking
Look out Mother I'm on my own
I was a dreamer once too
sighed my mother
small as a spider
on her long silken string.

Loaded

I've swallowed my mother.
Huge with her, I stagger, spinning
with the desire to sleep.

Each day she speaks to me
in my own voice. Each day
I shout at her, scaring the children.

I see myself as a child in a three-way
mirror: three faces out of control,
wild hair, myopic eyes that blur my vision.

I see a small, tight mouth that smiles
to hide its hunger. I hear her voice say, *Hold
your temper! Where's your will-power?*

Why are you so angry? I don't know.
I do my furious best to save the world; oh happy
world, waiting to be saved! Oh, happy me

if I can save myself from this need to be filled.
I empty the vacuum cleaner, hearing still
the angry suck and roar.

Bodywork

At twenty-one, swollen with all he has
consumed, been consumed by
he bursts his shirt, his shoes.
With more on his shoulders
than his three hundred pounds,
Bob walks alone.

His sixteenth summer
spent caretaking the island,
he photographed the empty house,
its driftwood walls and floorboards,
his rowboat on the beach.

Back home, he totaled the family car,
cut his leg on the sickle bar and tried
to electrocute himself on the
pump house fuse box.
He has become a bodywork man,

scraping paint from wrecks,
beating out crushed fenders;
resenting intruders, he slams
his truck around corners,
scaring the neighbor's children.

After all, he tells me,
this is a Private Way.

Day of Reckoning

The tub holds his body
in its porcelain embrace,
—steam rising, spring sunlight
aslant on the tiles.

Downstairs they are
laying out his father
in the Impenetrable Casket
padded with sateen;

his mother raises the lid
of the insulated freezer
jammed with food squirreled away
against a day of reckoning.

Where are the wormholes,
the rough pine box, the coffin
rusty with death
he saw in his dreams?

His mother opens the freezer.
His father lies in the box.
The tub holds his body
in its porcelain embrace.

Open

How can she be open about her needs,
so different from those of others?
Longing for the softness of her lover,
she takes each day head-on: office banter,
hen evenings, the uncomfortable chance encounter
wheeling her cart among the oranges.

She's tired of curious eyes looking and avoiding,
visits home: sisters with babies, husbands
exchanging looks, their impatient glances
urging *be normal, consider appearances.*
Her parents signal veiled disapproval, wait
for her to overcome 'unnatural passions,'

Out over the lake, across dark islands,
layered mountains heaped against the sky
form an ill-proportioned nude on a bed of water:
ludicrous breasts, too far from the domed head,
bump along the horizon; bent knees rise
from the flat belly, a cloud caught in the crotch.

How simply they lie there, she thinks, *the mountains.*
She, who has followed the strict path of her heart
wherever it leads and has felt the bud of herself
unfolding, floats on the pond of the world.

After

When you left me there, I didn't weep or dream
or put a record on the gramophone.
I wrapped the cheese back in its cellophane,
opened and shut the icebox, washed a spoon
and wished I were a little girl again.

appetite

Fig & Leaf

Young Wife

She doesn't see the unmade bed,
pajamas flung on the floor, her panties
left in a heap by the dresser, the mug
ringed with coffee, cold on her desk
until she hears his key in the door—
her mother's voice inside her head.

Trinidad, 1965

We wake early—watching
a lizard, belly to the wall,
wait by the open brickwork
for what comes in with sun—

woken by the clatter
of palms outside our window
when a breeze moved off the hills:
a sound we took for rain.

You on the sheet beside me
lie sweat-cooled, as the air
soft, heavy-scented,
slides in through the screen,

on this island where
it never rains till noon.
You reach to touch
my finger, touch one breast.

Motionless, I watch
the beating white throat
of the lizard as I lie there,
waiting

Coastlines

Palm,
hand, eye,
head, heart:
this is my coast,
the rock-strewn line
of my being: what you receive.

What I receive
is your palm
in mine, your line
of vision outward, eye
at rest, coast
clear. Take heart,

dear heart:
for what we receive
be thankful. You coast
here beside me, palm
my treasure, line
my garment and teach my eye

to rest, my eye
to see what my heart
knows of your coastline.
Then receive
me; hold me in the palm
of your embrace. Coast

with me down that coast
of both of us, where eyes
are cloudless, palms
together, and hearts—
hearts receive.

Deny the line
that separates us, line
on line of rollers coast-
ing in to drown us, to receive
us: head, eye,
hand, heart,
palm.

Fresh Figs

Thick-skinned, purple, large as my hand,
warm in the sun of the decadent Lido:
my father buys fresh figs from the man
who walks the beach with the soft, ripe fruit
in a cloth he unwraps for inspection: *"Fichi?"*
"Si, si," nods my father. *"Quanto costa?"*

Since then, whenever I see fresh figs
I think of my father glorying in them,
the hedonist in him at peace with the courtly
boy who thought first of his mother, bore
the weight of her private suffering, his father's
eye for women. I taste that Italian summer
in the plump, slippery fruit.

You wonder, love, at my delight in playing
with your body, uncovering the twinned fruit
in its single, wrinkled skin. I heft it in my hand, thinking
it's not just seeds that matter; I want
your strength to move with mine, your fig leaf
off, all your defenses down.

Mussels

Eating these soft lips
pink, fringed where they part,
—dark cilia once matching
the blue-black shells that shielded them—

puts me in mind of the smiling, blue
Lord Krishna painted on silk
and his nine delighted handmaidens in pink, orange and gold,
beside a river with lotus and waterlilies

—and of a picnic under flowering trees,
just you and I, eating mussels.

Moss Glen Falls

GRANVILLE, VT.

Up-mountain,
the narrow stream gathers force,
carving its way through ledge rooted with hemlock,
rubbing into gnarls and hollows
the layers of mica schist that wear like driftwood.
Then, swoosh of water,
as it laves and lathers the rock,
falling across it, falling against the grain—
the way at home the shower spray
runs down your lathered body, as unaware
of how it shapes the water as this stone
that bends the river toward the open pool,
an explosion so total, so generous,
there's no holding back.

Our ears too filled with thunder
to hear or think, I touch your hand
to show you the fern growing
from the rock at the fall's edge,
a wet, bright green.

Texas Falls, Early Spring

FOR GERRY

How green the river is,
stained by hemlock
rooted in those rock banks;
how gold it is, curling over stones
rounded by water's work,
the heavy rush and glide.
Stones sing in the river; mica flecks
like true gold in a frog's eye.

From the double-chambered heart
where pouring water delivers its turmoil,
the breath of winter rises.
We hold our breath and each other
swept nearly over the edge
by this miracle of outpouring:
a sustained melt and thunder
that enlarges the heart.

Stray

Yes, like my mother, I take in strays.
The orange cat, his ringed tail held straight up,
stalks round our back steps
as if he ran the place, rubs himself
against your trouser leg,
grateful for your disdain.

Rather than let him starve, I fed him
once I saw he wouldn't leave
no matter what I did. He stays outdoors,
sleeps in the sun, a huge
armful of fur— or climbs your car
to spread out on the warm hood, leaving
his prints on roof and windshield.

It drives you wild, I know, that arrogant
brand on the dust of the serious vehicle
that carries you to the world of work and money
where cats don't come out of the woods
bent on owning you. The way I figure,
it's a small price for being allowed
the simplest act of salvation.

Thanksgiving Letter to Friends, 1973

REMEMBERING REV. ROBERT MAYO

What do I want to tell you? That life's dull
in these suburban woods? Not true, though it might
touch you to think I thought so. I still
take on too many subjects, too many objects, blow up
balloons, ring bells, try blowing my own
trumpet, somewhat short of conviction. I disbelieve
in progress but think I might have made some: no longer
drop my pencil box as often, though I see my six-year-old
chews his shirt collar and shares his mother's
poor penmanship.
                              Were I a hermit,
as I often feel caved here in these woods, I would recite
your names as litany: *Edith, Elaine, Ariel, Marina, Richard.*
I dream you often: walk city blocks, climb
tenement stairways to find you. Hard
pulling things together, while all the while
there's a feeling of walking fences, arms outstretched.
I'd gladly fall, were you all there to catch me.
Crush mess is coming, with the proverbial goose;
I'm the one getting fatter, waiting
to see how I'll be carved once the bird
is off the table and into the soup. Who'll get
which piece of me this winter? Breasts, thighs,
wings. Do I have wings?
What I want you to know this Christmas is what
I heard my gentle friend and pastor,
a man of color, say from the pulpit:
Change your life. Do what you can. Give more.
I try. I've bought several cards
that say PEACE in five languages.
All their angels have wings.

The Search

In the search we have traveled
infinite distances toward the beloved,
believing our journey will continue to unwind
around the blue and green planet
touching now and then but never dividing
field from river, meadow from woodland.

We've been told that all divisions are finite
except division by zero, which is impossible.
All intersections are odd or even
and if you go in through a door
you must go out through a window
to keep the path clear and undivided.

You glide by me on smooth shoes
never stopping to tell me where we are in the program.
It's as though we were skating on a frozen river, black ice,
and the cracks that sound in the icy air
were the thunder of our thoughts, too ultimate
ever to understand or disobey.

It's the language of my dream you speak
and I must act or drown. If I stagger,
I lose the dream or the path, the hushed
silence of winter evenings, stars coming out in the dark.
I must stroke my way alongside you,
keeping in mind the goal, single, undivided.

The crowd in the stands applauds
shadowed among trees that bow gravely as we pass:
willows that bend toward mirrored tendrils caught in ice.
They are with us, the shadowed audience,
as long as they can see us, but they will
fold their blankets, return home to supper

forgetting what they have witnessed,
unsure of our message, ignorant of our mission.
It is pieces of themselves they will find,
the parts they left at home: fingers, toes,
sex organs, the left side of the brain.
They will think our search futile.

All they will remember
will be something about the river, stars
coming out. Zero will remain for them
the one true number, the number that divides
only itself, the distance we travel.

Appetite

Let's pretend we're not married,
that I live out here alone and you're in town
on business. You call from the airport,
say you'll catch a cab. Where can we
meet for dinner? I say, *Here*.

I separate four eggs,
grate a wedge of Vermont cheddar
and stir it with the yolks into
a white sauce: butter, flour, milk.
As I untie my apron, take down
two glasses, the headlights of your taxi
light the driveway.

You're at the door with
something in tissue paper:
How lovely! Asparagus!
As I whip egg whites to soft peaks,
you shave the asparagus;
we leave the kitchen
with steam and the souffle rising.

The asparagus heads are tender;
you pour the cold white wine.
There's something to be said for
appetite, the things we cook up together.

wall

Rabbit

November Cinquain

WESTON, MASSACHUSETTS

Morning
along our lane
frost clutches the bunched grass
Hunched among stalks my rabbit heart
pounding

The Wall

What is that wall? I never wanted it,
But somewhere around my garden I can sense
A barrier, once set down for defense,
Perhaps against the sea that fronted it.

It keeps the wind from blowing through my hair
As we sit close by peony and phlox;
It keeps my mind from fiddling with the locks
That hold me closed upon this garden chair.

"Giving is all," you said. But pouring tea,
Serving you cupcakes, not asking why you came,
I wonder, and yet know I'll stay the same
As I have been with you, and we'll agree

That it has been a charming afternoon.
The wall will be invisible again,
And nothing but your teacup will remain
When we have said we'll see each other soon.

The Terrible Baby

It's a parade! Children shout and point.
An enormous, pink balloon, the terrible baby,
floats in the sky above her belly. Ropes
hold it down. If it burst against the sun
it would fall, an empty skin, against her mouth,
shrieking as helium streamed out. Up there,
it bobs above the crowd; here below, she stirs,
restless; her belly jumps and pounds.

She wakens to a tightening that becomes
a warm, spreading pain. Her work begins,
her belly-work, to keep
breath riding the crest of every mounting wave.
Breathe in, breathe out. The rabbit on the ceiling,
splotched, ears askew, fixes her attention.
She floats on her breath. *Breathe in. Pant, now*
Blow! Blow hard! Don't push! Hold your breath. Now, push!

The head, a dark, wet patch between her thighs,
splits her. A sudden rush, a slippery
coming forth, and there, at last, he is,
her raspberry toad: legs, arms, fingers, face,
raging with life, familiar, kicking. Real.

Weekend Homecoming

All week the children dream of Tootsie Rolls,
waiting for their indulgent father. All week
she imagines dinner out, the intimate
picnic lunch, his body warm beside her.

Driving him home from the airport Friday
she can scarcely contain her excitement, chattering away
about how she fixed the toilet, coped with the broken fridge,
meaning to regale him, engage his sympathy.
He has his own ideas:

slippers by the fire, a candlelit dinner, not
frozen pizza and "I forgot the wine!"
Both want to be taken care of, a parent
there to greet them. Their parents grow old;
they're the caretakers.

Saturday morning. He's off to the store with the boys
after taking a shower; she stares at the soggy towels.
Crumbs stick to the breakfast mats; scorched egg
soaks in cold water. With all her heart she conjures him
back in the city, she at home with the children,
dreaming of his return.

The Observers

Outside the yellow house on the
Post Road, they are fixing
the water mains.

There's a graveyard there
with slate headstones,
toppled, venerable.

On the stone wall by the graveyard
the small child sits,
his mother near him,

watching the slow machines
scoop and clamor.
The trencher's yellow bucket,

a toothed jaw trailing sand,
dives and swings as it
dumps the heavy rubble.

Mom checks the ground
for the car keys, glances at her watch,
reluctant to drag him away.

High above them in the cab
the operator grabs,
pulls at the levers

with powerful, huge hands.
The afternoon sun
shines down from his windshield

flashing on the child, who looks up,
holding in his small fist
five wilted dandelions.

Mid-Way

HARVARD SQUARE, 1973

Traffic in the Square. I want to cross
here by the Bank where there's no light. I look
one way: there go my parents strolling off,
her arm in his, courteous, loving, firm.
I see them pass together through the crowd
of beards and beads that jam the narrow way.

I want to cross, but buses crowd me back
against the curb as I look the other way
to see my two small sons race toward me.
One catches my face with his sudden, brightening smile;
the other laughs upward, as if he hadn't seen me.
I open my arms to catch them, but they pass.

I'm cold. I need your arm across my shoulders,
But I don't know where you are. I look both ways,
here by the Bank, in the middle of my life.
There is no light. Just mirrors, mirrors, mirrors

Vermont Sampler

She looks up from the wrangle and whine of children
at hills that crowd in through the kitchen window:
rounds of orange explode there, softer than fire
among the green and golden pillow-heads.

Spruce and pine make little v's of shadow;
bare trees puff, smoke-gray, in windless air,
and on the mountain's warm, dark page,
a white fork writes "birch." She wants to capture

all the scope and texture of this perspective,
and with her sharpest needle, in fishbone, herringbone,
laid work, turkey work, French knots and seeding,
stitch it down.

Leaving the Children

VERMONT, 1973

We've left the children deep in their bright world,
metal cars curving across the carpet.
Through my streaming glasses your comfortable face
runs like watercolor, and I laugh to think
we've chosen this moment for our escape.

Summers ago, my sisters
would run with me out on the lawn
as lightning played over the Sound
and rain streamed through our hair, salty
from swimming, into our open mouths.

I'd do it now, peel off my hooded jacket, run
into the meadow, soaked and scratchy,
if you'd run after me, something
you're not apt to do. Wordless, you
tighten your grip. Hang on,

we'll slog back up the mountain to the house,
rain dinning our ears.

Nightmare

There's something I read I need to
show you, but all I can think is,
You should leave me for another woman.

falling asleep I raise the blinds
On a new landscape—bushes stagger to jungle height,
Blow to dust—*Is that her car in the driveway?*

The desert blooms poison spines, rain
sweeps away the sand. Changes flash by me
like colored slides— *Her footsteps on the stair.*

After you leave for work, as on
any other morning, I leaf through old
New Yorkers, looking for what it was

I wanted you to read: the story describes
how hostages, held in a bank vault,
become attached to their captor.

Marbles

Slowly, one by one, words like marbles
form on her tongue: smooth glass,
blues and greens.

She wants him to understand
her feelings for him, her sense of their
life together, the loneliness—

As she speaks, her passion
rises, words sing on her breath, eyes
shine, as she understands

as though for the first time ever,
just how she feels. Her words come faster,
shooting from open lips: jewels
fountaining toward him.

He sees her build an arsenal of words
and braces for the attack, fearing
her words, sensing their danger.

The force of her passion rocks him;
she takes his power from him;
he hears only the explosive "I need!"

Needy himself, he curls into a stone
and watches, fortressed there,
as balls of colored glass
shatter against his silence.

Mending

Bricks rot in our terrace wall, their red hearts crumble.
Feeling your in-turned anger, my held breath,
I walk our neglected garden through thick June air,
reading the inky squiggles etched in brick,
interpreting cracks in mortar, omens worked
by winter and ivy's creeping, sinuous hands.
Dampness eats at the rosy heart. I consider
how to right what's gone wrong in my house.

I wish the work were like a mason's:
hard but clear. I'd dig out piece after piece
with chisel and hammer, lay in fresh mortar, split
and place new brick, then open drainage holes
to let the rain flow freely across the terrace
into a garden orange and green with day lilies.

Tracks

like the ones that goes by our house, no crossing gate. My boys are there, playing nearby. Do I notice the train coming as I cross and see a headlight pale in the sun? Or do I feel the ground shake and know its presence by the rumble it makes, a sound that starts under my feet, not at ear level? I know the train is coming and watch the boys race alongside. I scream warnings. They seem so calm, so self-assured: Timo crosses in plenty of time. The boys scatter into the wood. There are lots of them, not all mine: companions, older boys. At least one is hunting. I know as I hear the shot: some animal they're after. The running boys are around me in the forest. I understand there's been an accident. Someone was shot, hiding in the forest. Another boy. Not my child. Not Timo. He's right here. Where is he? I don't see him. He's with the other boys. *Timo!* I call, *Timo!* He answers from the ground, propped up by his companions. *Mummy! I hurt.* Serious, not crying. I can't believe. Doubting Thomas had to put his hand in his Master's side. I put my hand on the dark spot that wets my son's blond hair. He has been shot. He's escaped me. If only he would listen, I could save him, but he will not listen. At seven, he's already beyond me. And I have given him: made the world a gift of my son. In my sleep I cry out at my bloody hand: *Oh no!*

> beyond our red house
> a rumbling in the woods
> white winter storm

A Woman's Place

My place is
>at the window
>looking out
>over saltmarsh
>toward the wider sea

My place is
>high on a rock
>on the nesting islands
>where sentinel gulls
>face the wind

My place is
>by my children
>leading them through the dark
>Pied Piper playing them
>out of the cave

My place is
>the cave the woeful
>dark to know it
>to move beyond it
>into light

You say my place is beside you:
>To keep me there
>you must walk a little faster
>keep up with me
>move on

carapace

Cicada

The House that Octopus

The house, that octopus,
hugs her to itself,
coils round her the false
arms of its embrace,
drawing her toward
its soft mouth, hidden beak.

Each tender gesture
once made with love —
cutting the bread, pouring
wine from the clear decanter—
pulled her closer, wrapped her
more tightly in.

Once she moved smoothly
over the waxed floor
spread with morning like butter;
now she scrubs at black ink in corners,
her life leaking like the freezer,
a slow pool.

The clock tells her the time.
It's Monday morning,
she's alone with her coffee.
In the closet, the vacuum cleaner
waits with its long hose
to suck her in.

Ironing

Once she has plugged in,
heated up the iron,
given up sunlight,
given over the time,
which flows through the dark
basement and steams
up from the flat board
running before her,
opening out like a road
—all six lanes crying
the names of exits
(Northeast/ Rising Sun)—
something about it
soothes, smooths out
the creases. In her mind
all roads run north;
snow blankets hills,
all possibilities
open before her.
White sleeves lift and flap,
smoke rises from scorched cloth,
a slow burn. Sole plate
streaked with rust,
the tiny holes weep
No Exits. Lucky,
she thinks, these days
most things require
no ironing.

Soap Opera

In tears over the dishes —lonelier
than she's been all day, dealing
with the dog, babies, wedding china—
the neglect her husband bestows upon her
seems held in this one moment.

She lets secrets out with the water;
her dreams of a lover curl
ghost-like down the drain. Folding
desire away with her apron, she leaves
to check on the children, turns

out the light. Later, she wanders
back to the kitchen, as if to find
something she left with her sponge,
picks up the sponge and wipes,
wipes the clean counter clean.

Deadlock, March

WESTON, MASSACHUSETTS 1975

Numbly we sit, wrapped in wool
waiting for leaves to unfurl,
for ferns to roll out their fiddleheads
and feather the woods,
waiting to release into spring,
into the nearly believable
carol and chirrup of nestbuilding,
the first green flush,
red smear of maple flowers.

Now, while the bones of things
stand out too clearly,
while the sun is stingy with its
warmth, we lose the habit
of imagining new beginnings, inflict
pain on others as numb as we are, unable
to imagine the knife
until blood runs, warm, down the blade.

Couple

If she had a place to run to, she would run,
her heavy body laboring for breath,
arms reaching, hair loose, streaming in the wind—
unkempt, unseemly, down some stony path.

Her weary husband shuts the bathroom door
to sit alone, wrestling with his bowels,
his sense of having failed confirmed once more
in the day's headlines, his monogrammed towels,

while she, his once belovèd Valkyrie,
caught, mired in the sucking river mud
of their closed life together, picks up her key
to walk the dog around the neighborhood.

Leaving

Leaving three
hamburgers on the table
near the ketchup bottle
the potato salad
on its bed of iceberg
the TV box in the corner talking, Mom
removed her apron
walked out into the field
where the sun's hot fingers
burned through her ten-dollar
bra to her nipples
and down she lay
among the grasses hearing
the katydids *she did she did*
she waited
for the sun to take her
give her back her body
root her to the ground
that she might
bloom

This Party

You came to this party
hoping to talk to Elizabeth Bishop,
but she's not here, so you
mumble to me instead. I came
hoping to compare perspectives
on a past we almost shared, to put
the past behind us, lay a ghost,
but you have erased the past. I feel
like an old friend, in fact, I'm an old
victim, feeding myself to you so willingly
you'd think I enjoy being torn
open, riven end to end.

Owl-beak and talons strike
through your feathered mutterings,
and I am blood on your snow:
a package of bones, owl-pellet
disgorged. I wear the old armor,
smile and say *Yes Yes*, smile and confess
whatever it is I have to confess.
You deprecate your work, and I
my style of life. Drawn by your brilliance,
your diamond facets,
I approach the bloody altar
and ask you for the knife.

That night I dream of dying,
of avoiding your weasel glance.
I hear the clock beetle tock-tock in firewood,
its carapace so brittle a fingernail could explode it.

Message

The table is red-brown marble
in the entrance hall,
the envelope plain white,
my name in your writing, unmistakable
in this unfamiliar place.

I'm sure the message is
something I don't want to hear;
whatever's there
I won't believe it. The word
Love, for instance.

Beside the letter, on that
bloody surface,
that polished oval,
you've left a small, toothed dagger
you say is the key.

Student of Sumi-e Desires Mastery

With brush and black ink
I could paint this August evening
on a soft gray paper sky

with black ink capture
the elm branch strung above us
red crescent moon

held between branch and mountain
hearing the cicadas
play the silence between us.

deep waters

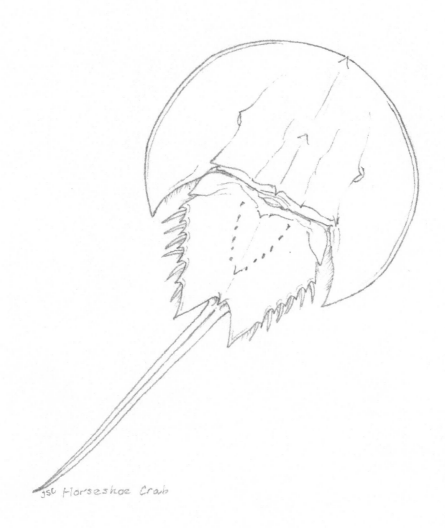

jst Horseshoe Crab

Early Morning Swimmer

My father hesitates at the edge where
gray glass breaks into cold foam, unwilling just yet
to commit his body, warm from sleep,
to that salty element. Under his tender soles,
sand grits and grinds, loose as liquid
where the wave sucks out. He wobbles, staggers,
knee-high in water, knees seeking a balance as he
wades deeper, trailing fingers.

Waist-deep he stands, divided,
legs and genitals at home below the surface,
chill tongues of waves lapping his pale belly.
He looks out toward the Vineyard—postponing the moment—
at the white blur of the ferry on its first trip from the Island,
the vague lighthouse cylinder at the far end of the beach.

As he wakes to the warming sun, sucks in his breath and folds
his arms above his head to take the plunge,
he remembers, as a child, tanned
from squatting at sandcastles dripped and pinnacled,
how he'd race down the beach toward the wave-line:
Torpedo number 3! Alert! Fire! How the cool salt embraced his hot
body, how he slid into it, slippery as a fish, fin and backbone;

he stands on a dock, bending toward dark water, his mother
encouraging him to dare the long inches downward,
arms plastered to his ears, coiled like shells. Aware
how fastened to the earth he has become,
he breathes out, takes the plunge, translates
into the new element, feeling the years
peel off into the new morning.

Master Swimmer

FOR BOB BARLOW

You swim through life the way you move each morning,
arm over arm, through the waters of Vineyard Sound.
You take its salty liquor in your arms, enter it fully,
delighting in easy command, your body's flow.
Watching the ever-shifting scene below you, you enjoy
the stroke and rhythm, freedom from tension and thought,
observer, athlete, and master that you are.

Only the stinging jellyfish alarm you:
flotillas of tentacles pulsing in the currents
raise welts on your tanned skin, could steal your breath,
threaten your control. So when the sun
and Gulf Stream currents bring the jellies,
you don your nylon 'sting suit' and seek clear waters
further from shore. Twice, proud of your prowess,
you swam from Nobska Point four miles to the Vineyard
and crowed like a rooster, to succeed once more.

I miss you, Bob, in these waters, remembering a time
when both of us in goggles, peering down
at sea stars, seaweeds, minnows there below us,
swam into each other blindly as, arm over arm,
we both embraced the element called life.

Bacchanal for the New Organ

SAINT COLUMBA'S, WASHINGTON, DC, 1981

On the long bench at the Flentrop
J. Reilly Lewis connects
fingers with feet, pipes with bells and bellows
to enter the ocean of J.S. Bach,
mining the deeps, opening, closing stops. Unstoppered,
the instrument pours forth treasure
as though no stop were needed nor even possible,
each braided line running clear as a rivulet over stone, running
to catch up, catch hold of theme, of resolution,
of whatever it is that stops the breath.
Our very breathing stopped, we hear
the music include, occlude and darken. Then,
before it can (we know it must) conclude,
the young Johann Sebastian
sits braced before us, embracing, re-inventing
Fugue à la Gigue, his flashing shoes
cutting up like a dancing master.

Phosphorescence

WOODS HOLE, AUGUST, 1977: REMEMBERING ELIZABETH GUILD LOEB

1.

Rowing at night, oars strike like matches against black water,
sparking the bioluminescence brought to Buzzards Bay in August
on the Gulf Stream currents. Even the clear comb jellies
that pack in near the wharf pulse with it, each transparent
body scribed in compass arcs by some luminous pen,
almost violet in the dark harbor. Swatches of light
follow each oarsweep as we make for shore.

Summer is ending. Tonight we sing
Bach's *Magnificat* in the Lab's new dining hall.
The village turns out for the concert, overflows the chairs.
As the strings tune to the oboe's A,
I look from among the second sopranos
at faces seen on the morning beach, the same
knots of families —scientists, students waiting
for Bach to take them beyond the wavy world, beyond
the sea stars, sea robins, dogfish and squid
they test and examine for clues to our very survival.
The music begins: fluent, alive, triumphant.

2.

In the collecting room, horseshoe crabs bump in the tubs:
limulus, ancient survivor, ancestor of spiders. Not a crab at all,
she swims on her back and crawls up the sand to spawn,
tank-like, eyes where they're needed, sealed in her shell.
My friend Betsy, the cellist, tells me how
one morning after a storm, she spent hours rescuing
dozens from above the high-water line. Two by two,

she carried them by their spines, flapping and writhing,
down to the water —only to see them half an hour later
making their patient way back up the beach,
tracing in wet sand the mark of their passage.

3.

After the concert, high on Bach and red wine,
we stow the cello in the car's back seat
and escape the hot hall for a midnight swim.
Stony Beach stands empty under a moonless sky
lit only by stars and a glow that is New Bedford,
distant enough to be lovely. We strip
and race down the sand through clear air, ready
for the smooth embrace of water, satin to parched skin.

I plunge, eyes open, and am bathed in phosphorescence,
the corners of my eyes weeping cold fire. It flows
from our fingertips, a tingle of stars, shower of
meteors, like the Perseids flashing above us, high
over Buzzards Bay.

                    Not even Perseus in winged cap and shoes
could fly as we fly, sparking shoots of pale lime light
but moving through the dark toward Medusa's snaky head,
his shield moon-bright, he must have felt
the power we feel, caught
in this otherworld-miracle: light without heat.

We wonder aloud about how the earliest fishermen
to waken these luminous micro-organisms
—nets drawn through moonstruck water,
spears thrust toward a silver back—
must have called it a god-sign, that flash of fire.

In this moment, we float unshielded, in a
softshell stage of our crabbed existence, lie
on our backs like children, kicking up luminous foam.
Remembering how once we made angels in snow, we make
glow-angels, flail arms and legs, laugh aloud in the starry air.

Suddenly, from the parking lot above the beach
headlights blare out. Four dark figures move

across the sand: "Hey, girls! How'sa water?"
More taunt than question. Pinned
by the blind light, we squirm away in a slow crawl,
but the searchlight follows and the water
flashes its tell-tale fire. How absurd to be almost forty,
caught in the act of play!
                              These men could be creatures
from some other planet, harnessing Earth's energies
to their own infernal uses. Their searchlight
is the only light they see by. Their world
is what we call the real one, the one we must return to:
Betsy to nursing at the city clinic,
I to house and children, suburban lawn and pavement.
Each body will take its proper place, our views
assume the usual perspectives—except
in moments when the discipline of practice
pays off and the phrase of music lifts, the line
lifts, released from the horseshoe shell.

We leave the water, nonchalant as possible
under the jeer of headlights and four pair of eyes,
hoping our age will show and disappoint them,
refusing to be robbed of our pleasure.
Wrapped in towels, we enter our own safe car,
her cello our awkward, backseat guardian.

Regatta Week

PLOCKTON, ROSS-SHIRE, SCOTLAND, 1972

At low tide the harbor
is otter-brown ground
by Dal, the blind end of the village,
where whitewashed stone houses huddle
like sheep in changing light
under steady rain.

There is often rain
as sailing dinghies moored in the harbor
prepare for the Race. A light
breeze at the start is grounds
enough for the sailors, huddled
in oilskins, to sail out from the village

and try for the Trophy. The village
watches the colored sails form a bright rain-
bow, fan out from the huddle
close-hauled, leaving the harbor
for the squalls of Loch Carron, around
Seal Island, where the light-

house no longer lights
a herring fleet home. The village
tells tales of ghosts there, ground-
less stories told to keep a firm rein
on the children, who harbor
no illusions, but row out to huddle,

play Spin the Bottle, or break from their huddle
to raid the orchard, playing like seals. Some light
up a fag before rowing back to the harbor,
to the sharp eyes and tongues of the village
where gossip falls on their ears like rain
on indifferent ground.

Indifferent to this place—where, tonight, grounded
at low tide, clinker-built hulls lie huddled
below the seawall in a fine evening rain
as the victors head pub-ward in the soft late light
of summer—those children will leave the village
for continents far from this harbor.

Unchanging ground, changed in a headline's light:
OIL IN THE NORTH SEA. The huddled village
watches as rainbows arc across the harbor.

Secrecy

hides in dark waters,
holds onto his knowledge:
the yellow throat bulges
with what he knows.

Thin green lips take in
sunlight, blue sizzle of dragonfly;
the long tongue snatches
wherever his gold glance rests.

Only at night, where mallows lift
pale heads by the salt pond,
sounds the deep eruption
of all he is keeping.

wings

Grackle Feather

Foggy Bottom Morris Men Dance for the Economy

WASHINGTON, DC, 1981

Togged out in knickers
belted at the knee
these bureaucrats and lawyers
bounce and pound
or twirl in a slow caper, lifting
white flags of handkerchiefs
over bowlers pinned with silver.
Children shriek with laughter
as the Fool, claiming he's Mother
leaps down among them.
The dancers face each other,
hoot, shout, clash staves
which, swung off-rhythm,
could crush a skull.
                    Engaged
for once in a wordless battle
of breath and muscle
fought without memo or brief,
they work to increase production
having been taught
the higher they jump, the higher
our corn will grow next season.

Caged

NATIONAL ZOO

The Monkey House echoes, clanging,
empty of crowds this rainy afternoon.
The spider monkeys scream and spit, springing
from wall bars to ceiling bars, down
to the floor, where they fight over apples.

The young chimp nibbles his fingers; his swing
hangs limp in the rank air. Pressed against
the front bars of the cage, he stares
morosely at the woman who stands before him
carrying a folded plastic umbrella.

The woman speaks aloud to the child ape,
Who simply sits there, fingering his chin.
"Look!" says the woman, raising the clear umbrella
slowly into the air. A transparent bubble
blooms in the space above the woman's head.

The chimp's long fingers curl around the bars,
his eyebrows startle, and he raises his head
watching the bubble fold, open, fold
then open again, till, reaching
a thin, hairy arm through the bars,

he jumps up, up and down, eyes shining,
begging her, *Do it! Do it again!*

Snow in October

She thinks of her lover as snow falls on the city,
comes down with enormous arms, embracing trees
whose boughs bend under slow weight, as if beauty
itself bowed down in honor of the light
spread over the bed of the city like a sheet.
So he has taken over her bed, her life
with his great arms, his overwhelming body
—or so she wishes, at times, she might be taken.

How alive she feels, watching the huge snow
stop everything by changing everything
as the city yields and glows —but she will waken
to the scrape of shovels and, wakening, will know
that groceries must be bought, the carpool driven,
and she must fight this brightness, this takeover.

Long Distance

Hi there, I've started this conversation. So now what?
Do I ask you how you're doing, are things okay
across that ocean? So hunky-dory that
you won't want to talk to me, don't have much to say.
Do I ask if you miss me? Confess how I miss you?
That brings up the question of how we'll ever meet
again, and when: a delicate question, a bit too
tricky to approach directly. Let's be discreet
and stick to everyday matters: the leak in your roof,
the children, how big they're getting, how much they eat,
how near you sound. How dear you are. How far
we now sit from each other. We must be brief,
yet silence falls between us. Dreams are sweet:
pelagic longings echoing in my ear.

Aubade

Don't tell me, love, that you must go away
since life without you isn't life at all:
a room without a picture on the wall,
night starless, dawn diminishing to day.
When morning slides its light across the Bay
and papers are delivered down the hall,
don't tell me, love.

Keep me illusioned with each word you say,
tell me outrageous stories; make me feel
that of all women I'm most beautiful.
Hold me, touch me, teach me how to play—
and if you love me less than yesterday
or five or fifteen years ago, be still:
don't tell me, love.

Leave wordless, then. Though I would have you stay,
I hear a voice as if from some control
tower announce your flight—a final call—
from this bright bed where close to me, you lie.
Don't! Tell me, love.

Absence

Away from you too long, I walk through days
like stepping stones along some mountain path
followed without thought, care or breath.

I swim through hours, treading water,
sleep, wake, and sleep again.
Moments quicken, weeks slide by.

It's as though I am the one absent,
the one gone missing, waiting
only to reappear, breathe you in again.

Approaching Forty

At home in my body as never before,
I dream less often of being lost
in subway and hospital corridors.
Friends enter my dreams, bring
messages. The sun shines clearly, revealing
the pattern of hearts in the lilac bush,
the singularity of oak. Each face I meet
opens distinct, not blurred, as once I saw
any beyond my safe circle.

At some point in my fortieth year
I stopped wondering if you still loved me.
We have settled into one another
like parts of an old sofa, sagging a little,
letting go. I can finally tell you
what I hardly knew myself until I said it:
I'm glad we're together, hanging on
like the avocado plant in the kitchen window:
rooted, leafing toward sun.

Witch Birds

With a soft clash

      of feathers, like rain

          or palm leaves in wind

      the flock of grackles

lifts its single mass

      rises and folds

in a gust

      rushes upward

a black silk fan

      of wings.

Of Tutankhamen's Tomb

Behold
Deep under stone
The gilded triumph of a Pharaoh's face,
Mask within mask of gold.
From under stone
They fathom up and finally uncase
A crumbling cup,
A brittle casque
Of bone.

waking

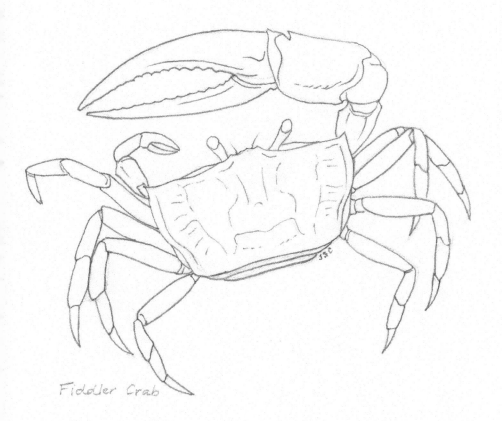

Fiddler Crab

North Wind Sonnet

Why sit indoors this high blue day to write
hunched over a machine? The scudded sky
above the saltmarsh where the tide runs high
is swept with wings clearer than any slate.
A halyard slaps against the aluminum mast
of my small boat, insistent as a bell
calling me not to worship, but to sail
into the open morning while it lasts.
Greedy, I want to cleat this moment down—
the wild careering of our circling blood,
the freshening gust that lifts us through the waves—
so that, when fog slides in across the Sound,
when neap tides suck the saltmarsh down to mud
and the wind turns east, I'll have it as it was.

Meditation

WOODS HOLE, FEBRUARY 2017

Washing the dishes,
I watch how a week can vanish
under the sluice of days.

Down the warm staircase I hurry
to fetch the trash can from the driveway,
where all day it languished as I sat caged indoors.

Hit by the frigid dark, I glance up, struck
by a blaze of stars, fat, brilliant, dazzling my eyes.
High above Vineyard Sound

broad-shouldered Orion strides
with his sexy sword. And, there, flung overhead,
Cassiopeia's Chair, throne of a Queen!

With the Durrells

FEBRUARY, 2020

Waking from deep slumber
to tossing trees, wind
shaking the window, bright sun,

he thinks, at eighty-five, he's
not at home, but on a warm Greek island
—the one place on TV

that transports him from the
weakness and confusion
of the body he now inhabits,

the world he wakens into with
reluctance and a wry
smile: *I thought I was in Corfu
with the Durrells.*

Great Harbor Salt Marsh

WOODS HOLE, 2019

At ebb tide, the shallow water
mirrors grass blades black at the base
with mud that sucks and sings,
nourishing pale ribbed mussels
and fiddler crabs that hole in at high tide.

A skitter of fry leaps in the shallows
as a green heron, low among grasses,
draws back its snaky neck to nab the unwary.
A pair of egrets, feathered ghosts,
dart in for quick pickings.

It's late July. Sea lavender floats
its pink-gray cloud of blossom,
and crisp, green shafts of *salicornia,*
those salty succulents, wait to be found
by kids who collect them for pickles.

When those children, grown, bring their children
back to the village, will this small marsh
now sparkling with stars
still be here harboring life,
reflecting the changes?

Would its absence even be
noticed? One minor link
feeding, sustaining a planet
we've earned no right to claim,
to call our own.

Whale Factory

FAIAL, AZORES, MAY, 2004

Salt rimes dark rocks at the tide line
below the whale factory
tucked in the left-hand corner of a bay
once red all summer with the blood of flensed whales.
Stripped, boned and gutted,
their great bodies were fed to fire, their precious oil
poured from stainless boilers; the stench each night
belched from the German factory
over the town of Horta, home to Azorean whalers.

Today, across the bay, Horta's tiled roofs glow
burnt orange against a hillside of patchwork fields,
as, strangers on tour from other worlds, we swim
and laugh in blue-green water, the sun our furnace.
Later, lounging on black volcanic sand
beneath a lava cliff rough as cinders, we wonder
what gives this water its salt; why it stings so,
drying on skin.

Violence lies silent below us, waiting. Times past,
volcanic shudders blew open one side of the island;
rivers of flowing fire boiled the waters. Could seismic minerals
mixed with this bay's blood give this water its extra salt?
Or perhaps, for all we have done to Earth or failed to do,
perhaps the briny bay that took us gently
into its arms this May morning, was born —like the Twin Lakes
in the Caldera on São Miguel— from the tears of gods.

Today, Vineyard Sound

OCTOBER, 2006

As the sun rises this morning,
I watch a ragged congregation of
cormorants swim, their snaky necks
zigzagging across the still Sound.

One lifts itself up from the water,
rattling black wings,
another flies in and brakes feet-first
to join the croaking flock.

Swimming, I see, above my low horizon,
on the far stone jetty a solitary
figure stand rock-still, his rod and line
fine threads glued to water.

In all the peace and glory of this morning
I think of Gaza, of Lebanon:
families caught, tangled,
like dolphin in long nets

not of their making.
Arm over arm, stroke by stroke,
I feel in my throat my own helplessness,
a croaking voice rising.

Hearing News from the Border

MARCH 2, 2018

After all, we're all exiles
from other times or places,
longing for past Edens
where we know our
minds and bodies belong.

Not all of us are refugees
fleeing imposed terrors:
violations still recalled
in shame, that bitter herb.
We can only just imagine

how it feels to be the occupied,
disrespected, a being whose soft
privacy has been invaded,
whose deepest self
destroyed. Our orchards

taken from us, our anger
disallowed, merest needs denied,
from place to place we run, exiled,
seeking some other Eden,
snakeless, secure.

Horseshoe Crab Molts

VETERAN'S DAY, 2019

Helmets litter the beach, glitter
in the cold light of morning, as a sandpiper
squadron flits across steely waves.

No far-off thunder
this autumn day, but the War we were born into
floods back: the lumbering planes

with their heavy cargo;
explosions heard some nights
beyond the Vineyard; the sand

strewn next morning with silver scales.
"But why do they do it, Mummy? All those
fish no one can eat!"

In the newsreels, marching helmets,
the lumbering planes,
the heavy price.

Waking, Woods Hole

SUMMER, 1981

Enter this clear morning like a swimmer,
dive into its perfect wave;
mares' tails sweep the sky on a north wind
above the dark Sound, crisp with sails.
Past those stiff triangles ferries throb and cross,
frothed at the bow, foam-waked,
headed for islands that shape our horizon.

What the eye hungers for, lungs take in—
great gulps of morning, the laundered sky-smell.
Joggers move up the hill toward the lighthouse
rejoicing in easy limbs. You too
can dive in, enter the touching air,
or, left behind some wall or sealed window,
miss out on the fanfare of morning.

Putting Away the Boat

The mast's dead weight across our shoulders,
we gather in the shrouds,
the trailing stays,

and with slow steps, past red sumac
where poison ivy glows
and beach plums darken,

we form a cortege for summer, turn
backs to the beach
to shoulder winter's burden.

The sadness we hear
in the cry of the Canada geese as they vee south
is our own, not theirs.

MARY SWOPE—New Yorker by birth, Cape Codder by choice and family tradition— has followed her love of language in poetry and song since childhood. A graduate of Radcliffe College and The Harvard School of Education, she has been an elementary school teacher, poet in the schools, worked for two years in children's book publishing and later as an editor with a nonprofit poetry press. For almost 20 years, she assumed a leadership position helping to develop The Washington Revels in Washington, DC, and has been named its Founder. She studied Scottish Gaelic, won awards in Gaelic song competitions and performed at festivals with a Gaelic folk group, MacTalla. She still sings in choruses and choirs, and loves to swim in the salty waters of Vineyard Sound. She was primary Editor of the anthology *American Classic: Car Poems for Collectors* (SCOP Publications, 1985) and her poems have appeared in a variety of publications, including a chapbook: *The House, That Octopus*.

JULIA S. CHILD is a biological illustrator and natural history artist. She works in pen and ink, colored pencil, half-tone techniques, and watercolor wash, and her work has appeared in more than a dozen books and numerous scientific journals and textbooks. She lives in Woods Hole, Massachusetts, where she teaches popular classes in drawing plants and animals to students of all ages.